IN MY OWN FLOOD

IN MY OWN FLOOD

CHRISTINA STRIGAS

IN MY OWN FLOOD
Copyright 2016 © Christina Strigas
All rights reserved.
2nd Edition Copyright © 2022

No part of this publication may be reproduced, distributed, or transmitted in any form or by any means, including photocopying, recording, or other electronic or mechanical methods, without the prior written permission of the author except in brief quotations embodied in critical reviews, citations, and literary journals for noncommercial uses permitted by copyright law.

For permission request, email the author.
christinastrigasauthor@gmail.com with the body:
"Attention: Permissions Coordinator"

All art illustrations in book by Christina Strigas

Interior layout by Maureen Cutajar
www.gopublished.com

ISBN 978-0-9951865-2-1

CANADA CATALOGUING IN PUBLICATION DATA
Strigas, Christina, 1968-, author
In My Own Flood / poetry by Christina Strigas

I dedicate this book to two men in my life who have been there for me and supported me: my father, Peter, who taught me how to see past the ordinary; and my husband, Greg, who treats me like I am extraordinary. Thank you for your light in my dark.

This book is also dedicated to all the Greek girls and women out of Montreal. To all the Greek boys and men. To all the grandmothers and grandfathers. To all whom I can touch through words.

Thank you. Efharisto. Merci.

Dear readers,

Thank you for supporting my love of words and entering my poetic world. I do not proclaim to be anything but a woman emptying my soul through words. Every page can be read on its own. Every poem has a life of its own. All poems could be a continuation of one or none at all. I found it difficult to organize them, because my mind is always in different paths; hence they are written as a book with different parts. There's a story everywhere I look; some in my head, some in my heart, some in my soul, some with the dead.

Thank you to my family who have supported my writing and let me be true to the artist in me; especially, when I locked everyone out, and when they came back when I opened the door.

I also want to thank you, the reader, who purchased this book and still believes in the magic of poetry. Thank you for your support. To all of my friends and the poets I have met through social media sites, thank you for believing in me when I didn't believe in myself.

All artists go through self-doubt, it is part of existing within other realms of reality. I have been writing poetry for decades, and within this book you will find some new poems, some old, and some that were hidden in journals… All for you to read and enjoy. Human emotions are so vast—like a forest, an ocean—nothing can truly capture its essence, but I hope you connect to my words and thoughts.

Thank you to all of my muses, in human form and other.

— *Christina Strigas*

CONTENTS

PART ONE:
I will write an epic poem one day
    The Week Starts on Friday / 3
    I can't wait until you get the real me in a room and lock the fucking door / 4
    Whisper Secret Poems / 6
    I Would Like… / 8
    Unknown / 9
    The Road / 11
    Hospital Love / 12
    Tide / 15
    Soaked in the Rain / 16
    Enter / 18
    Epic Poem / 20
    Hanging on a Boy's Arm / 23
    And Then / 25
    Sunlight / 26
    Charades / 28
    Break My Fall / 30
    Periscope / 33

PART TWO:
How poetic are the lines in the palm of your hand?
    Elements / 37
    Poetry / 38
    Thoughts of How You Break My Heart / 39
    In the Moment / 41
    In Simple Words / 42
    Seduce Me / 43

Portal / 44
To Be a Poet / 45
Kiss / 46
Past Lives / 48
A Sonnet / 49
Another Sonnet / 50
Sonnet 3: Art / 51
On Being a Poet / 52
I Thought / 54
Heartbroken / 55

PART THREE:
Montreal is the call
Soul Tapping / 59
My Gift / 61
Empty Space / 62
Clouds / 64
Pour Toi / 65
I Wore It for You / 66
Back in Time / 68
Walk / 73
Soul Mates / 74

PART FOUR:
Goodbye after walking three months along the wall of China
It's Been a While / 81
Streams / 83
Parts Long Gone / 84
Don't / 85
Focus / 86
You Think / 88
Unwritten / 89
Star / 90
Exit You Missed / 91
Voices / 94

Those Familiar Leaves / 96
Ninety-Seven Years / 98
An Ode to Steve / 101
Missing / 103
In My Own Flood / 105
NYC 2013 / 106
So Feverishly / 108
One Thing / 110
Shades / 112
How I Fell From The Sky / 113
Follow Up Poem / 114
Four / 116

PART FIVE:
Internal Riots

Use me as a motif / 119
I used to / 120
To Love / 122
I don't want to know / 123
Brand New / 124
Black Sharpie / 126
Surrender / 127
The Fire of my Storm / 129
Spilt Wine / 130
Reasons / 132
Sanity Chased Away / 134
Ageless / 136
Spell / 137
On Call 139
Making Love Vs Fucking / 140
My Oxymoron / 141
Full Moon Riding / 143
Calendar / 144
Black Sheep / 147
Burns / 148

Real life / 150
In the Middle / 152
Poems / 153
GNO / 154
Metropolis / 157
Trashing / 159
In the Bones / 162
I bear words / 164

Acknowledgements / 167
About The Author / 169

PART ONE

I will write an epic poem one day

The Week Starts on Friday

My first poem will be the one
you will adore.
I slide between words
like a wet pussy whore.
No, it is not smut
I write for you,
but a long forgotten moment
when you wanted me spread out

your own one night stand slut

pursued and perused.
Your family portraits are darts,
mine are a fuse.
Together we make no love,
our words abandoned like orphans.
No more perfumed rhymes to hide
the ugly. It's here. I am alive
ready to eat you up. On my
knees, as usual. Enter my sin,
you make me proud with your
sexy lies and automated
deletions. Never say never.
Always say always. Welcome
to nonsense. Welcome to my thighs
and please do not distinguish
between the fake and real color of my eyes.

I can't wait until you get the real me in a room and lock the fucking door

This was my morning thought,
evening thought,
and everything in between.
The washing of the dishes,
the love songs of anonymous names
and misspelled heroes.
I think in random notes.
I fold the tiny piece of yellow
lined paper and make each day
a new love affair. You wanted me
once, up against a hotel wall.
You wanted me twice, inside the
washroom of a famous café. You wanted me
three times at six in the morning
before the sun rose on November
eleventh, the year too close to forget.
I'm not that stubborn, it's true.
You gave up too quickly and believed
my no's. You thought I never lied. Then
you thought I was the best detective
in Montreal. But you hide so well
in satellite pictures, I especially liked
the photo
with your wife
who was quite lovely. Not sure why
you would ever cheat on her.
You looked so content and she was
blurry, out of focus. I think
we should still lock the door
and you should ask me
why
I never left you behind.

Or do you know
the answer to your own questions,
you arrogant man.
And do you know
that these are the reasons
I run? Truth makes
me uncomfortable. Uneasy.
Sleepy.
Lock it already, and do not
forget
the candles and the songs
you said you would play
in the dark corners of my mind.

Whisper Secret Poems

Do I owe it to you or not?
You carved
our initials
into the tree trunk
to make us real,
more than a poetic metaphor
in the back seat of a car.
I should call us
visual artistry
but your deep fodders
of underlying waves
have been left in
the bottom drawer,
under the panties
and jewelry boxes.
Consonants and one clap
syllables
are connecting us now.
Periods separating
our flow. Forests
drowning our echoes
as only the animals
can see our
initials now.
Were your parents
sheep or wolves?
Were you raised
by none of the above
or all?
Does it matter now
or did it matter more then?
Deep secrets you whisper
through poetry

and songs, that have
more meaning
to strangers than me.
Once I listened,
then the conjunctivitis
was cleared and my eyes
saw past the grin,
past the sex,
and I ran
as far up as Mont Royal
mountain took me, as long
as my tired legs
lasted. My heart pumping
sadness, words escaping
my breaths, sentences
piling up like sweat.
All those questions
I asked you, you
never replied
with the right answer.
You lied.
You changed your name.
These little things
I can't forget. I'm
not into head games.
Love stays loyal. Mock
me by putting me down
no more. Poetry is
in my blood,
not disloyalty.

I Would Like..

I would like to think that you trust me more, but I see you don't.
I would like to think that you love me more, but I confuse my desires.
I would like to think that you ache like me, but I feel you less.
I would like to think that you pray like me, but I fear you have another faith.
I would like to think that you want me badly, but I'm left alone.
I would like to think that your mind is free, but I believe it's taken.
I would like to think that you think of me, but all the doubts plague me.
I would like to not think, but alas, my mind never rests.

Unknown

In the damp night
your kiss
would take away
all the ache
of yesterday.

In the light sky
right before the sun rises,
your arms
would caress the scars
which lie invisible to the eye.

In the twilight
your body would possess
mine,
begin where I end in time.

In the middle of the day
your words
would make all of
the mundane disappear,
a smile from ear to ear.

In the time between time
your mere existence
would be all I need
to get by my blocked fence.

In the universe
I could be the clouds
and you the sun,
and I would not want
it any other way.

Even if you argue,
digress about my dress.
Our minds are above
each other's
in the grips of
the unknown.

The Road

I read no more
as I once did.
The love you take
is on my sleeve.

I see it all,
so clear to me.
You think you hide
but I see through.

I know you want me
on my knees,
to give to you
what I refuse.

You soon will walk,
forget my soul.
I see the road,
before you go.

Hospital Love

Lying in bed with my eyes half-open,
the night at the emergency
was no Saturday night party
still surrounded by painful souls,
swaying from one body part to another.
Read one hundred and seventy-four pages
of the book I told him about
could not finish that horrible, trashy romance.
Atrocious writing and the romance was a baseball game.
But my mom sat next to me;
between chapters,
reminiscing my childhood.
And I remembered the reasons I love the way I do—
everything seems clearer with no sleep.
Pain
at four in the morning.
so we barked about Medicare
but thanked the doctor as if he was God,
and my mom said
this country has gone to shits.
We never waited nine hours to see a doctor
(and I was not alone).
Yet how that smell makes you feel
like you are so fucking alone,
and young Chinese doctors
holding my future
as I lie naked
staring at my mom
as if I was five again.
Then we giggled
because I told her the onion story.
When the pain from inside manifests
and you don't care if your poems rhyme

or if they are truly poems
or confessions.
Beautiful lies, Charles calls them.
And I reread that line
a few too many times.
At least I have fifty cents
for a phone call.
Being off the grid
watching my phone and tears
land in the bathtub
was not a highlight.
I think that Charles and my mom
were quite the audience
to my fall.
Sometimes the people
that you think
love you the most
turn out to love you one eighth of their own capability.
Their love has all these limits,
like kilometres or mileage
or distances
on a highway.
I speed too much,
I love too much,
I get speeding tickets
other people follow
while I'm on the verge of losing my license.
As I fall asleep on my mom's shoulder
you creep into my thoughts.
Don't be so surprised
for you never give up (like the rest).
When you find your way in,
bring a candle
to the empty table.
There is no electricity.

Old-fashioned virgin love
(not like the rest).
I am not fully ready to empty out the pockets of my soul.
I just feel different.
You must know.

Tide

There are all these sides
to you,
still unattainable
yet pulling me in
like a tide.

The truth is, you make it all better by simply existing, breathing,
 and living.

Soaked in the Rain

When he blocks his ears
to the questions
and tells me nothing
I want to hear.
When he thinks his answers
are the only ones
that I may fear.
These are the times
the ocean calls,
right about Anne's age,
the moment all my falls
are storming in on my rage.
Disclosing nothing,
pleading the fifth
to your assumptions on my wings
floating above the waves.
Hiding it under the rocks and things
that will be meaningless one day.
My kids will give parts of me
to the poor
while your letters burn inside my own door,
a ray
of
sunshine
in the shadows.
For you are mine
on land, sea, and water.
In every part of my soul
in which I falter.
I am yours
but time may change
the air,
age may block your stare

but a soul
continues its journey
always beware.

For I am soaked at the park
in the rain,
or maybe not,
for the lies
should
remain
beautiful.
The truths
equally mysterious.
So do not ask me
when I write
or why,
just stand way back
and watch me in my jeans
as I make a Greek cup of coffee,
and all the rest
will never matter.
You will avoid my best
and cease to jest,
as I cry on your shoulder
and you place my strand of hair behind my ear.

Enter

I do not have to meet you anywhere,
but in my mind
where the roads are in construction,
the gravel dangerously bumpy,
ditches in surprises,
Montreal potholes in abundance.
Those bloody detours; confusing,
anxiety ridden,
misplaced and I am letting you in.
Welcome.

You enter graciously, carefully,
confidently.
You have no difficulties,
no fears,
you actually like it.
You want it.
Of course, I think you
saw way too much.
So I crumble,
move my lips to no music.
Stay a while.
You ease into my answers.
You like my hard nipples,
trashy romance,
smoking, drinking ways.
You enjoy watching me read,
crossing my legs and
concentrating on every word,
comma, period.
You buy me the booze,
the drinks, the smokes
and then you hold my

hair back as I purge it all.
And still,
you kiss my neck,
and erase all of my memories.
I call you my vampire;
for I forget the crash,
the death,
the loss.
I thank my angels I'm alive.
Protector of angels,
they come in threes
and hug me.

Their tiny arms loving me.
I cry for the hope they gave me.

Pour me another glass,
I tell you quickly, sadly.
You understand.
You buy me the bottle
and refuse to say no to me.

You know I would meet you
anywhere and nowhere.
You know how to enter and exit
like a king.

Epic Poem

"I will write an epic poem one day,"
I say.
One fine day. When the ache
in the chest overtakes
the sunshine and only a touch
from a lover can heal. You have
a way of sliding under the radar,
slithering onto my skin
while I am not paying attention
to the hockey scores. The grip
on my heart is bound
by words that replay in my
head, a fever that stirs my
body. It guides
me to leave cherished words at
your doorstep as a gift so that
when you rub your sleepy eyes
from a dream, you will read me first—
think about me first—before you
splash your face with water.
In the grips of you
I sleep, and wake among the lost
children who have no vision
of desires buried deep.
You,
the man who had unfolded all of
me—this poem is for you.

A fear within me builds towers
high enough to fight all the soldiers
struggling to break them.
But only you have succeeded.
Only you have brought me to my knees,

your name—your beautiful fucking name—
on my dry lips. You must know that in my
mind, I was made of marble. You dug so deep,
cracked me,
unraveled
my virgin skin waiting for you.

So I climb your body, swim backwards,
save lives, read you poetry in bed,
write, write, write.
And you say I'm infectious.
I don't really listen to your compliments,
I think about how I wish all my words
could be soft, tender—but I know
that eventually the dark takes over.
Tosses me, breaks the gentle girl within
and when you sense the storm
you lock down your windows tight,
but I am already inside.
You hate me then. You want me out.
You cry for my release, which I give you
and then you want me back—even for a
day, a second, a minute, anything—but I
know this will never be enough, so I wish
for you to feel my words like rose petals
on your sleepy eyelids
rather than
bullets in your heart. My intention is to stand
in front of you and block the wind
the way my Pappou did when he
walked me to grade school in the
Montreal wind. Nothing felt safer.
I wish for you
to place a scar on me with your words, enter my inner walls.

I want to be lost in your poems,
see my reflection everywhere.
Am I selfish?
Yes.

"Is this your epic poem?" he asks.
"Not sure," I say.

I am breathless many times
feeling the divide between us
part as I run toward the night sky.
If the ocean can accept me
I will freely dive, never come back
a human. I will stay underwater,
turn into a mermaid,
a nymph,
goddess of the sea—
anything but this battle
within the mind and soul.

"This could possibly be it," he adds, after reading the last line. But I knew I could do so much better.

Hanging on a Boy's Arm

The day has become the night.
Enter the man
who reads me,
creates me
into his favorite female character.
I waver, fall
over his words. Tripping
over them, bumping
my head at this catastrophe
of a situation. Bending
my will to further
explore the bottle of
booze empty at my feet
as I contemplate breaking
the glass
that holds no answers
to my never-ending pursuit
of the imagination.

In the silence
you set me free
among the
wolves. You
should know my
weakness
is all of
you—your
faults, your
power
that ties me to you.
You can fill up the empty
space around me
when I am alone

of in a room full of people.
You showed me the way
to my soul.
The path
was filled
with debris,
fainted curses,
hollowed promises.
Yet there you stood
with nothing but
a bouquet of words.

And Then

First you drove me home in your friend's car.
I wrote your number with my
eyeliner and then it smudged.
I forgot your last name.
Then I saw you driving
and we swerved.
Parked on the side of the
road and talked for hours
about mundane things,
while thinking other
thoughts. And then you took
my hand and we went to the
park where I used to swing.
You said
"I want you to be the mother of my children."
I laughed.
You did not.
"I'm serious."
These thoughts became my
thoughts. This love became my love.
And then I hated you.
I threw my compact makeup case at you.
You loved the color green and its warped effect
of misunderstandings.
I ran home at 5 a.m.
I became everything you wanted me to be
and then
you altered my world
with one kiss, one
look, one touch.
And all is forgiven, forgotten, misplaced.
And then you tuck me into bed.
My silver streaks your path
leading to my secrets.

Sunlight

There is no
sunlight here, only
the type of fish
that are so dark
your own will
shine bright. I am
not scared of how
you throw words
of hatred like stones
in a river. I am
not threatened
by love. I can
bask in it for a
while, take my
body and rest in
the six
thousand foot
ocean.
You must know
how water affects
me. No I'm not a
fucking mermaid, and
I'm not a nymph. I'm
Me. No sunlight
without you. You bring
it to me. Your poetic
words of love as
you caress my skin—
spoken poetry, slam
poetry—you have it.
That gift that drew
me toward you all
those years ago

when I was on the
edge of seventeen.
So many have tried
to enter through the
cracks (there are always
cracks)
but you, alas, have
my soul next to you
every morning and
night as our
legs touch in our
sleep and our
children
open up our
eyes to the
beauty
we created.

Charades

I'm pretty good at charades,
beat them all with my gestures.
I'm Greek so I move my hands
when I talk,
break open beer bottles
with my hand.
I may seem all sweet and nice
but I could hurt you.
Mostly with objects
you can never see,
hardly noticeable
from this distance.
But naked in my bed
you could twist me
around in seconds
and see that my tears
are on the
pillowcase.
I can pick the charade words,
select the perfect movies,
actors,
sayings,
and let the games begin.
Make a mixed drink that makes you
want more.
Select a playlist
for somber moods,
haunting moods,
slide an adjective over my body parts
and I'll come up with something.
I hate parts of you.
I detest the fatal flaws
that will come between us

like a scaffold.
I think in ancient
times and read scripts
in my mind that you dreamt
about so long ago.
I see through
you, past you,
and still
I want to see all the parts
you hide.

Break My Fall

I close my eyes.
See the words floating around,
trying to find meanings.
Placing them together,
apart.
Walk into me,
crash my world
with your car,
to read all I think about
and all I don't.
Lay into me,
feel all I dream about
and all I forget.
The Universe is vast,
but you are in the same
spot every day,
close to my star
with no name.
We glance at each other
as neighbours do,
protect our homes from thieves
who steal your soul
and spit it out
for others to step on,
to stick under a shoe.
You can catch my words
as they copulate toward you,
but you do not grasp
what is torn in pieces.
You cannot glue the paper
together, the words have been
scratched out,
for no one to read

or to reread
the tragic escapade of our lives.

There is less to say each passing rainfall,
and less time to say it in.
I forget the way you smile at a joke.

You leave me standing on a cliff,
peeking at the river below.
If you want to push me,
I am awaiting the pressure of your hands
on my back.
You speak but you never say
what I need to hear,
so let me fall
into the blue that beckons me so.
I will not place stones in my pockets
for I truly don't want to succeed.

I have always wanted to be a bird,
or a horse,
don't you see?

Spread your morning jam on
me, eat your sweet tasty
breakfast so the berries can
burst
in your mouth.
I will still be
a disappointment after
you lick your lips.

Break my fall,
turn me around
with your strong arms

and
make me a butterfly
instead. You have the magic power
to turn me into the dust
in the corners
of your room.
How low I feel
when my feet touch the ground.
My skin is like a plastic table cloth,
I lie,
I make up the past.
Turn me into the song
you listen to
over and over again.
The one you said was "ours."
It's calling my name
through the speakers
that only I can hear.
Continue your daily torment,
put on your black tie
to open the door.
Go to work,
as I am already gone,
with my arms spread wide
wondering what to cook for dinner.

Periscope

You look at me through your periscope,
see my different shapes.
First I'm in range of your breath,
I am near enough for you to smell
the fried oil on my clothes
and hair,
and then I am on the outskirts
of your love
trying to find my way
back to your eyesight.
But I sway in and out
like a pendulum
and you abandon me,
restless and morose,
lovesick.
I love you without boundaries
or categories
and I'm still traveling
to salvage,
disprove,
my intuition.
Now I'm at arm's length away
but you are still searching for more
facets of me
when all you have to do
is open up my crumbled papers
in the wastebasket,
only
you can't be bothered.

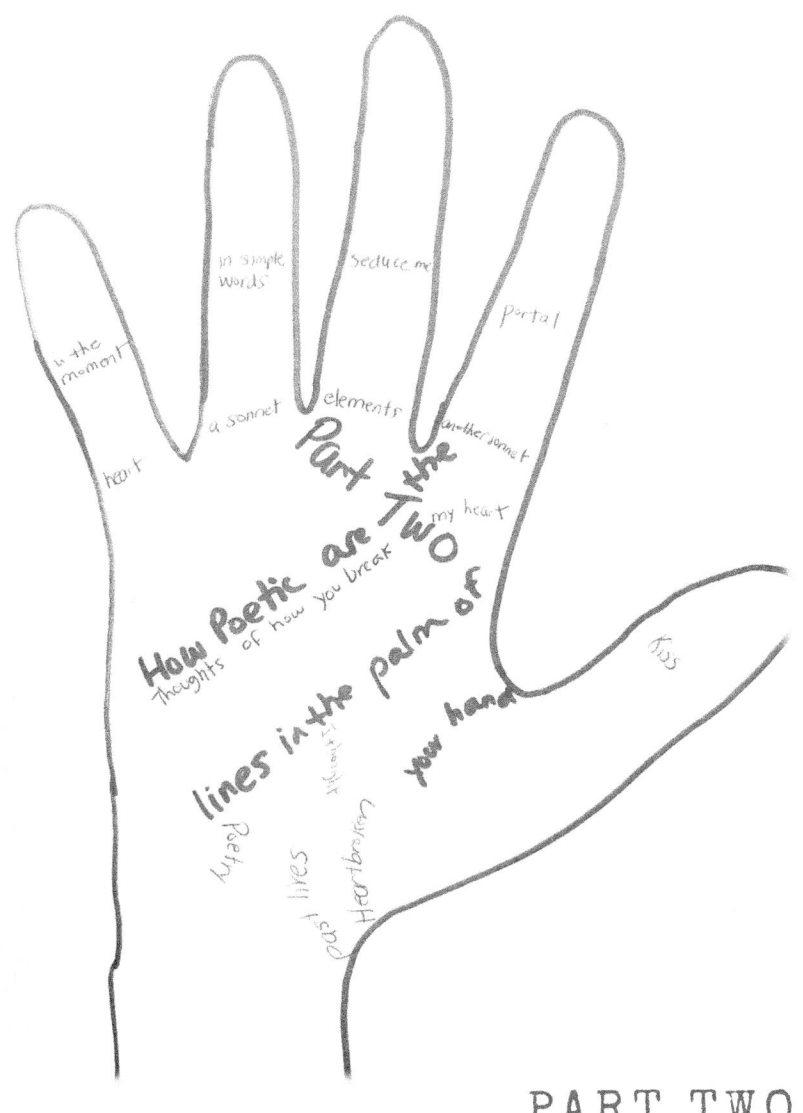

PART TWO

How poetic are the lines in the palm of your hand?

Elements

It is not how
the sun rises
but the color
of the sky
at dawn,
dusk, twilight
that I marvel at,
more than the necklace
in a green box
of the tiniest butterfly
captured in my drawer.

Poetry

Poetry is not meant to be understood
like clear water.
Think.
Reflect.
And now
perhaps you see
how
it passes right
through you.

Thoughts of How You Break My Heart

1.
When you said
to live in the moment,
I knew
that I was
the only dreamer
between us
willing to
travel through time.

2.
If I had to pick
a time and a place,
it was how
the angry wind
replaced your sweet
baby blues
in the middle
of Times Square.

3.
The way you tell me
how I feel
before I know
myself.
The way you
bite my neck,
hold my waist,
before I feel
your touch.

4.
Fuel the
mind first,
then the
body second,
then the soul
has no
choice.

5.
You said the wrong words
when I wanted to hear
the right ones
and this
I cannot forget.
How
you complicate me
in your trapped mind.

6.
I'll fall apart for you.
Stitch myself back
together before your eyes
close and the wind's song
becomes ours.

In the Moment

Right now
you can read my mind
because I let you.

And every page says to dream—
something that is not as easy
as it may seem
to most, but
it comes like breathing to me
as I talk to my favorite ghost
and he tells me how he had
all the knowledge
at the tip of each edge.
He gently showed the way,
paving the asphalt along the way.

In Simple Words

Some people think
writing poetry
is a waste of time.
Others absorb words
like young pupils.
Still others have their hat on
and
walk right past us.
It may seem like a breeze,
a simple tune you hate,
that may have taken days
to compose in the heat of the muse.
All these wonders,
most of them skip tracks on life;
you do not need to hold my hand too closely, I've always seen it.
So perhaps it's time to tell you
that
I will always love you.
It may be simple to say,
but we both know
how writing this
and saying this
are polar opposites
in both worlds.
It is somehow in all these places
on Earth
we visit,
reminding us of
the one we love,
no matter
which ocean
we look out from.

Seduce Me

With your poetry and words from a long forgotten era.
Attach bits of my soul to the commas,
float near my aura through
space, connect my broken parts
with pen strokes.

I ache for more.

Flatter me and taunt me
like a hunting snake.
Open up my word bank.
You know exactly, precisely,
what to say.

I am a mess,
a sleepless lover.

I feel the emptiness pour out of me
wherever you are not. In my dreams
you are there. In my wake
you are there.

My soul is not taking no for an answer.

Portal

Open up your portal.
Lead me into
your golden streets
and grey walls.
Laugh at all of my witty jokes
and comments.
Keep up with me.
Give me a comeback—
adjectives, nouns,
anything will do.
Show me your ugliness.
I will embrace it
as long as it is a part of you.

To Be a Poet

To be a poet you have to dig deep
with a shovel.
Have a ciggie,
drink some booze,
and let the pain explode.
You have to show your wounds
and French kiss
up against a wall.
Break your heart.
Hold it in your hands
and watch the blood
drip down.
Write till your eyes can't see
words anymore.
Listen to your favorite
song over and over again.
Speak the truth
that others can't,
and wave it around
in front of the ocean
where you skinny dip
till your skin freezes.
And watch the sunrise,
waiting for your muse
to arrive
so you could handcuff
it to your bed.

Kiss

Skin to skin, we reevaluate our lives.
Little fingers and toes are between us like knives.
Come ride with me and have a cigarette.
I'll see to it that it will be your best ride yet.
Or stay at home and watch another rerun of Happy Days.
I'll tell you all about the hot sunshine rays
as they burn through me under my skin,
which you wish you were beneath in a faraway Country Inn.

It could be all in my brain waves,
not connecting properly during all these wicked
raves. Blood-red eyes create delusions.
Beer bottles break in these dismantled illusions.
Walking down that runway
with dark blue makeup and high-heeled boots of grey,
she is dangerously attractive,
more than I could ever be in this life I
live. I should fall at my own feet and quiver
but I shall not let my body shiver
or be part of this tragic vocabulary.
It makes my insides weary.

Do I ramble on incessantly?
As you decipher my need to flee
this day, hour, minute.
I'll explain it to you if only we could have a moment to sit
and discuss the emblem of this family.
Do you like silver or gold crests? Really,
answer the questions ahead.
I feel a headache arising, I'm going to bed.
I hate to talk to myself
when everything is turned off,
but the voices keep on awakening me,

my hand reaching for the paper and pen to see
how far I could continue without sleep
and thoughtless words inside me leap
to own the page and hear it crinkle,
knowing that tomorrow's sun brings another wrinkle
upon my face.
And he has no inclination to take a finger and lightly trace
the outline of my lips,
or press his body close to my hips,
at the click of a light
I feel no kiss goodnight.

Past Lives

My hair was red
like the wine in my glass.
I had a garden full
of red roses
and I lived in a medieval castle.
I was an Indian chief
with animal feathers
around my head.
My tribe vanished before my eyes
and then I was walking in India
and you were born
before my eyes.
Your mother died
and I took care of you.
Now you are my son.
My daughter was my mother,
she is here to heal all our
bruised wounds,
to unite our spirits
and dissipate our sadness.
I played the piano.
I wrote letters
with a feathered pen.
I walked the Irish plains
and healed many souls
from Ancient Greece
to Irish villages.
And my love,
you stoned me to death
when we were slaves.

A Sonnet

If ever anything was true for me
It was your vision I once dreamed about.
It is the way you arose from the sea
And entered my life filled with more self-doubt.
The changing direction of the soft wind.
You walked with a confidence I once knew
And left your footprints wavering behind.
You spoke with a whisper the faint breeze blew.
If ever anything escaped my life
It was the words you uttered that bleak day.
You might as well stab my heart with your knife
Than abandon my ocean so far away.
I scraped my knees on the sand covered beach
Crying out for a touch, kiss or a reach.

Another Sonnet

Let us think of a road far off our path
Where we could walk holding hands in full view
And not feel the hatred of others wrath
While the letters remain in my pocket too.
Love will be aflame along the grey road
And a subtle caress will become law.
On your back you will carry my full load.
Sensing the drive in me is purely raw.
The streets will be silent, full of false hope
While our fingertips travel each other's skin.
If we walk away we will stop at the rope.
Reach the line that tells us we can never win.
Here is one last warning thought for your ears
There never was a road filled with these fears.

Sonnet 3: Art

The art that surrounds me is in your eyes
You can feel the brushstrokes from where you sit
I can mix the colors to create more lies
The people can swarm us with their wise and wit.
Walls are exploding with canvases
You never showed me how lovely you are
Now I am aware of all your paint messes
And I aim to finger paint you from afar.
The selection of flowers and still life
Is speaking once again to my sleeping soul
That will awake once your wandering wife
Is finding her Truth at a Rabbit Hole.
I can analyze the colors you choose
While you moan and cry about painting the blues.

On Being a Poet

What does it really mean to be a poet?
Is it when I look up,
or

D
O
W
N

or side to side,
and you snap a picture and post it
on that awful Facebook site
that has brainwashed society?
Do I look like a poet then?
Poets are hard to find
    search under pebbles
    in the sky
    between two walls
We are hiding from the
camera with our tattooed arms
    and hearts
    bleeding out alcohol
    and forgotten cigarettes.
I am on the beach
    &
    I am wearing a poppy flower
and w o r d s
are R
    O
      L
        L
          I
            N
              G

out of your mouth
    too quickly
for me to write them down
and pretend I made them up
for one of my poems that is definitely
NOT ABOUT YOU.

To be a poet you have to stick your hand in your heart
and write really hard with the other hand
on vanilla crème paper bonded with glue
and a fancy hard cover
that someone gave you as a gift from Indigo.
To be a poet you must hurt everyone's feelings,
including your own.
To be a poet it is essential to read other poets and wish
you had come up with their poems first.
It is SUCH
a lonely place with no windows and a view
and shutters that refuse to open.

I REALLY DO NOT KNOW WHAT IT MEANS.
All I know is this:
I copied out all my favorite poems on graph paper
lined paper
toilet paper
any paper
and by twenty-one
I realized I had a writing disease called poetry.
It can never be cured
so I was told
the w o r d s
kept on fighting with my immune system
and I hate most of them.
I swear I cannot control my brain from **SCREAMING** out.

I Thought

I thought my language of love
was poetry,
but when I met
you I was tongue-tied.
From across the room
our eyes met,
and I realized
I met myself.
Words crumbled
as your lips
pressed firmly
on my hand.
You were a perfect stranger
whispering hello.

Heartbroken

I imagine you kissing her.
Whispering all those
sweet nothings,
the words
you said to me.
I saw your picture
the other day,
her face was blurry
but you were
holding her close.
I swear
I could still hear
your heartbeat
breaking me apart
every day.

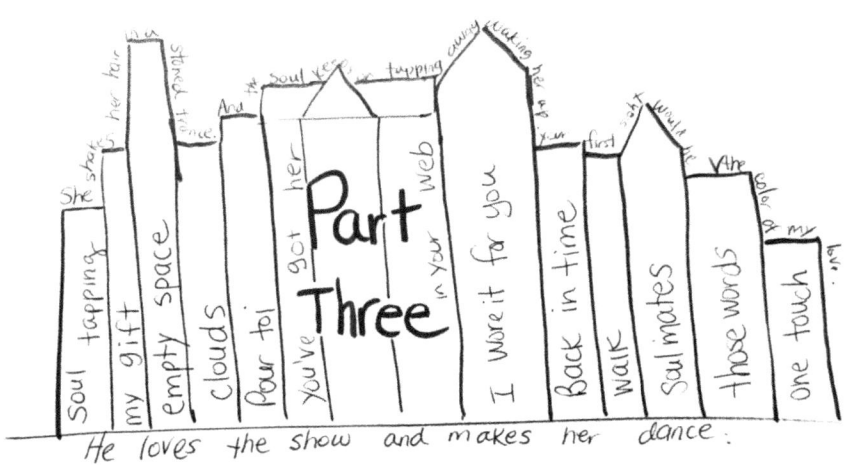

PART THREE
Montreal is the call

Soul Tapping

It is the tap of the soul
that ignites the mind,
the body close behind.
And when the paper runs
out the words never do.
In my sleep they scream
and shout,
always on the united screw
of the interlocked worlds
scouring about.

It should not take
much to spread her legs.
Those words, one touch,
you've got her entrapped in your webs.

At least she knows trauma
spreads her internal drama
all over the kitchen table,
in sexy New York aprons
with no underwear
and tons and tons
of unmarked cars peeking in her lair.

He loves the show
and makes her dance.
She shakes her hair
in a stoned trance.

She has to cook,
buy protein shakes,
read her favorite book.
with nipples erect,

continues her bakes.
And the soul
keeps on tapping away,
waking her up.

My Gift

If I had a way of controlling the morning sun,
I would rip it from the sky and
place it just above your bed.

Upon opening your eyes,
your first sight would be the color of my love.

Empty Space

Woke up to your sounds,
some kind of growl
similar to Ginsberg's Howl,
when magic gloves were something wacky
yet
poetry still did not mean a thing
as the Beat Generation continued their song.
Except me and the few
that saw those portals open unfamiliar
senses and sounds
of lost loves and words so profound,
our senses were alive
with the realization
of how tulips lived and died
and the beauty never lied.

Fancy that you, baby, can comprehend
how my love rides
on tulips' wave—
their intensity, purity,
their unspoken poetry.
Every word erased
is replaced within my soul,
sprouting spring seeds
in the middle of Fall.
The letters in your name
as magical as mine
are to you,
so strong, full of inner fame.

These words are from my pages,
pondered on ink
then let loose on thumbs.

Tiny screen aches,
morning solitude,
pre-dawn dates,
taken from my cup
to yours.

My doubt is grand,
but when you hold out your hand
my faith sees the stairs
to your magical door.

I believe every blessed word,
tantalizing and pure.

I cross out and rewrite now,
too much thinking
on a full moon
night. Now it is day,
now mine & yours.

I sleep, I wake.
I wake, I sleep.
And there you are
smiling at my return,
watching me
watch you,
watching you
watch me.
This perpetual need
to be as One
and cease this infantile run.

Montreal is the call
as you wrap yourself
around me
in this empty space.

Clouds

Above the clouds you float
in grey,
cool slacks
and attire.
Hovering high,
filled with facts,
trivia bytes,
ghosts travel
among us.
Past lives,
recent quotes.
Songs that shine
between us
like brilliant diamonds,
stones stay far
under the untouchables
while we dream
of being closer.
Crawling up staircases
in the sky,
you, the eagle,
I, the raven
for the dark crashes
inside us,
the strength within,
the artistry between
the invisible lines.
You take nothing away
but give it right back,
packaged,
just for me
and I accept it.

Pour Toi

How many soul mates can there be
can we see through walls
break our falls
carry on and break the chain
mend the love or let it rain
numb ourselves with music and words
ignore the sign of the birds
wear sexy dresses
and get in these loose messes
listen to the wind
the ink flows like a river
never freezing in the winter
binding time and sex is always on my mind
wth you
with me
in us
making such a crazy scene
lost in the in between days
and constant sunshine rays.

So I step back
lose my track
and dive in the river with my clothes on.
Catch me head on
you have strong arms
wicked charms
only a kiss can stop me now
you know exactly how.

I Wore It for You

Come and see me
speak the language of fools
and court jesters.
You cannot miss me,
I will be wearing
my bright midnight-blue
hand-made scarf,
thrown over one shoulder
and barely touching my exposed back.
You say you are too occupied
with road signs
and rubble.
Excavate out of your site
and take a stroll
down my avenue.
I will leave the door ajar
and not be frightened
by your notorious knock.
Aye, I may be blindfolded,
hoodwinked,
misinformed.
Or I may be
enlightened,
accomplished,
proficient.
You will be the scholar
and I the pupil
to this ignoramus life.
All I want is proof
that you have loved me.
No matter how illogical,
inconsequential,
or adrift you are.

Plead your case before me
and let me be the judge
to decide if your evidence
is worthy,
or if you have any.
I just want you to listen to my words
and compliment my scarf.

Back in Time

1.
Darkness prevails before you go.
You said you would not do this.
You said you could not do this.
Yet something happened before
dawn. I dreamed you were near.
I dreamed you were so close, I could smell you.
You were wearing simple shorts and a t-shirt,
outside it was snowing,
and you told me, "I am in love with you
and have always been."
I tell you,
"I know and have always known."
You tell me,
"Come over here so I could see you better."
I tell you, "I can't move right now
and I don't believe you."
You tell me,
"Believe it always, no one else is
you but you, no one else has your eyes
but you,
Could you walk away now?"
You walk over to me now and touch my face and
trace my lips as I stare at your mouth.
We kiss
and I wake up again.
Time to make coffee and toast
time to forget the dream.
I have to run to write it down, I say to myself.
Try to remember it
and I'll revive it when I need you most—
like now,
like later,

like tonight,
like driving,
like living without you.

2.
You seem to be the only one
yet are not.
The possibility is endless
of unlocked doors
and locked windows.
The castle is so high,
sometimes I think you'll never reach me.
The steps are so grey and your touch is still absent from mine.

3.
Seeing you again,
talking, laughing,
exchanging words that no one understands,
leaves me drained once again.
Your broad shoulders feel fresh to my touch.
I heard what you were trying to say to me
but chose not to.
I pretend you mean nothing to me
while inside I am alive with so much passion.
I want to share your drink,
every touch is a message,
words do not have to be uttered.
I know the sad life you lead.
I could touch you in ways that are boundless,
an unanswered motion
responding to your inner call
that I swear I hear.

4.
Once I heard the name Alejandro
and thought if only you were him.
I would meet you at
cafes,
restaurants,
parks,
bars,
cars,
motels,
telephone booths,
old-fashioned carriages,
fancy hotel lobbies.
Let your imagination join mine
in these meetings of astonishing heights,
jump on a horse with me and run
I know it just can't be done.

5.
Last night I thought I heard your car outside
but nothing—only empty roads appeared.
Still darkness and my unnerving thoughts
remained unbearable
to not wrap my legs around yours
unconsciously in my sleep,
and close my eyes as you close yours.
I do not see you for days,
weeks, months.
Yet when I do
I can't breathe,
I lose myself in your presence.
Your eyes haunt me
and make me feel understood.

6.
My heart beats,
my legs move,
inside I am fidgety
to speak to you and look at you.
When the moment arrives
our eyes meet
but nothing else must be seen.
I cannot hide from your glance.
Awaken me, I am asleep,
and I will let your hands
slide up my blouse
if you will
let me do the same.
You say the wrong words
and I retain everything.
I am an artist.
I look exquisite.
I am a writer.
Sheets are wrinkled,
walls are holding me up.
I can fall
into your madness
of pills, alcohol,
transparent glasses,
drops of coffee at the bottom of your cup.
You try to escape every day.
You are running so absurdly
as I chase the air
and see the wreckage remaining.
I smashed my car
thinking of your arms, cheekbones.
Yet every night I see you as I write.
I feel your innate power
over my hand,

this pen,
this second and now it is gone,
forgotten for a while
as my eyes
travel to another sea,
so rough and so dry
to my peeling skin.

Walk

You are so stable
in this pure love fable.
You walk towards me
and see what I see,
an empty shelf with no books
lacking the waterfall and the brooks,
you ask me to take a walk
so all we can exchange is senseless talk
about architecture, nature and the sun.
The vastness of it all; the futile run
to catch ourselves
insistent, lonely at the lake
overlooking the trees and acting for everyone else's sake
as the scene is ready for act one
and at the moment you ask me, is this fun?
To walk with you alone at last,
pick a flower before this too becomes the past.
I want to respond
so honestly about our ominous bond
but we must turn back now
and stop these questions of how.
How do we find the way back
when we left no crumbs on our track?
Let's continue this walk, you say.
Where will it lead us today?
Perhaps to another city
where you wouldn't look at me with so much pity
and you would be my hero, my labourer, my
man my direction, my song, my passion.
Instead you are none of these, yet all of these.

Soul Mates

I'm walking down the Main Boulevard.
You see me
and stop.
You open the passenger side door.
Do I want a lift?
I say, okay.
Your car smells of Pinewood
and cigarettes
(drops of coffee stains).
Your mirror is cracked
and your poignant cologne
intoxicates me.
I want to hear so badly what you were thinking
when you first saw me,
instead
I ask you what song is playing.
You don't know.
The conversation starts.
"You have to help me.
I need your advice.
I love her
but she loves him."
"Who?" I ask.
You press on the brakes.
I almost missed the stop sign.
"Are you okay?"
"I'm fine."
"What should I do?"
"Tell her, call her
I know I would want to hear."
You glance at me.
"You are really so easy to talk to."
"That's what I've been told."

"What perfume are you wearing?"
"Something from Lancome
I don't remember the name."
"It's nice."
"Thanks."
"I want you to hear this song."
You insert a cassette and press play.
I listen
and I really like it.
We're approaching my street.
"You want to go for a ride?"
"Sure."
You drive around
and we smoke a cigarette.
"Do you think you could love two people?"
"Probably," I answer.
"Have you?"
What do I say?
That I've loved you since first grade.
"No, I haven't," I say.
I look out the window.
"Me neither," you reply.
Tell me something
"Do you believe in soul mates?"
"I think there are many types."
"What do you mean?"
I flick my ashes,
they fly right back at me.
"I think there are love soul mates,
brother soul mates,
sister soul mates,
music soul mates,
book soul mates,
art soul mates,
father soul mates,

mother soul mates,
friend soul mates,
and probably children's soul mates."
You are quiet.
"But what do I know?" I add.
"You know more than you think.
You know how I feel."
You park.
You look at me.
"Am I one of those soul mates to you?"
"Which one?" I reply.
"Any of them, all of them?"
"I can't say, do you think you are?"
You bend and gaze at me
"I feel we are connected.
We are all connected."
I dare not meet your eyes
You reverse and drive
off. No more words.
You didn't like my answer.
You stop in front of my
house. You wait for a few
seconds.
I say "Bye.
See you around,"
but it's summer
and I don't see you around.
Boulevard St. Laurent is calling.
Sometimes I think I see your car
or your eyes.
Sometimes I think I hear your voice
but it was so long ago
I forget how you spoke.
I can't find you anywhere
I should have said

Yes.
I was one of your soul mates.
One Hit to the Body
is playing on the radio
and that's the song
you liked.
I actually love that song.
I bring myself back
to the moment
and realize
you were talking about me.
I was the one you loved,
but I was with someone at the time.
And I turn up the volume.
Life is full of riddles.
I managed to figure one out
a little too late.

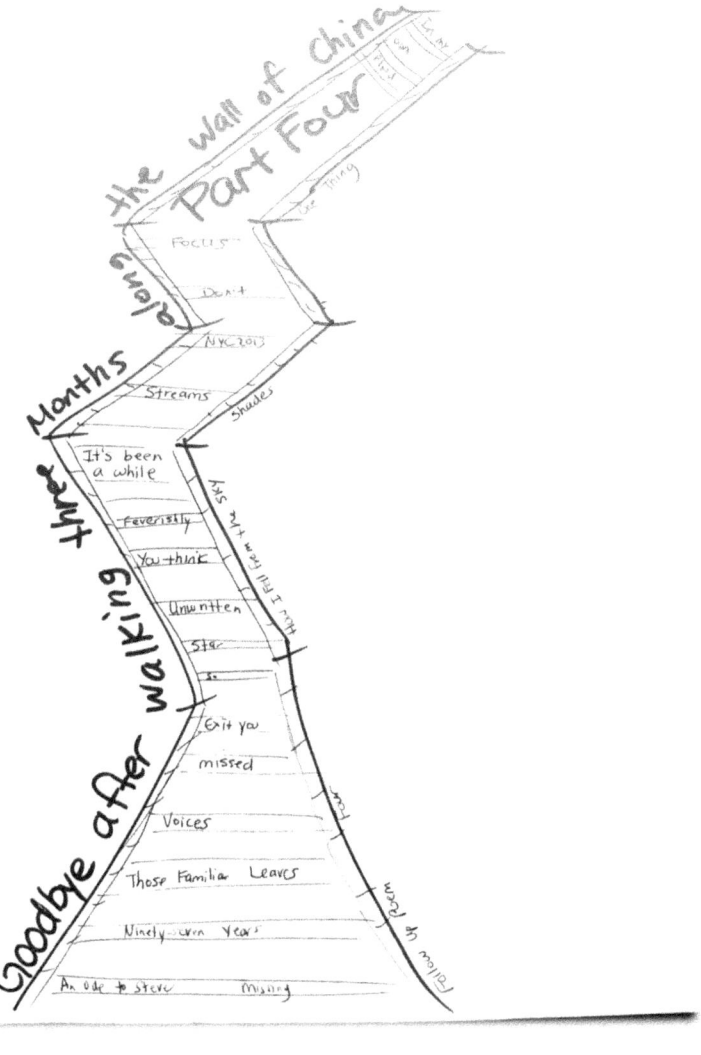

PART FOUR
Goodbye after walking three months along the wall of China

It's Been a While

He says he loves the way
I do irrelevant things
and then he takes it all away.
He doesn't read me anymore,
much less see me,
and the windows
are finally sparkling.
The forest has those paths
and you see what I see,
if only in grasps of straws
for that moment,
and that's enough
for a while.

If you think there is no more
heartache inside of you,
you are mistaken.

Just when I think
my life is misplaced,
I start again.
I can't speak for you,
or him,
or her,
just for the poet
and not the muse.

I am too simple
and complex
in one sentence,
imagine up close,
shattered dreams,
illusions,
hopes.

Just know
it's never about you.
It is how the silence
between us
has become
too comfortable.

Not sure if this is much
of a poem,
or thoughts,
or the combination
of both,
or the artist
putting on makeup
to go to dinner.

Streams

I do not know
if there is a truth
to words astray,
how the stream flows.
We stare at time,
wonder
how motives, ambition,
passion, and sex can drive
us into killing
deeply
like a blade of words.
A sword of our love
as we swing,
slash
in the downpour,
walk to the chirps
of the cardinal bird
then I look to my left.
1977
signs everywhere
of you and I
in heaven.
Dead Kennedys speak up,
your crowd is dwindling.
Mine has forgotten the path,
searching for the latest trends
while I relive the old wrath.
Trekking to Mont Royal,
taking the gravel road
to the Cross.
Again
the same initials
scream out at me
and of course I wonder,
you would too,
What else am I left to do?

Parts Long Gone

It was not only
the car crash
that broke parts of me,
made me some kind of hero.
It was my heart of glass
as it shattered at the door
when you swung it open
and kept on asking for more.

Don't

Don't garden my moods,
don't put up my sex for sale,
don't swim in empty pools.
Walk with me in the city forest,
see the branches on the buildings,
hate all TV
and urban words,
slam me with old English
and forget the poetic slang.
You cannot possibly know
or do this for me.

Don't do it for me,
don't make me out a liar.
Don't woo me.
Just forget my language,
heritage,
my art has many muses.
You are too nice
under that roughness
and I am too rough
under my niceties.

Focus

Do not look at me
or pretend to see me in the night.
Do not want to hold my hand
or squeeze my waist tight.
Do not slide your hands
underneath my thin pale blouse.
For I am on the run
from my own private house
from locked diaries, burned
up souls.
Enter the hash-tag whores
with perfect tits and scores.
Better to never know my skin's moon,
I am off tune.
A giggling fool
always misinterpreting the rule.
Red carpets, free drinks, flowers,
stepping stones.
Falling between the lines,
landing in ditches
as you slide your hand up my thigh,
losing control of the wheel
on a furtive high.
My desire on your tongue
as you let yourself finally feel
every part of me I hung.
Do not look at me.
Let me explode in my own dust.
Let me wallow
about my lack of trust.
Let me imagine your dark eyes
full of lust
as I run,

run,
hair flowing
not in a bun,
up to the lookout at Mont Royal.
Examining other people's initials,
recreating love stories.
Up all night tapping with the furies
to forget how you
gave me chills.
I run down the hills
as the sun sets,
and still
your name
turns out to be
the poem of my life.

I run
to be free of you
and realize
I am,
for I never had
you at all.

You Think

Just because you say "leave me"
I'm already out the door.
You think because I'm sleeping
I'm no longer awake.
I look at my white ceiling,
find my words and connect them
dot to dot in my head.
Midnight snacks and packs of lies,
relentless pursuit of you.
I'll give you up
and your brutal words
can squeeze my heart no longer.

You think you're the only one
who suffers,
who is bad to the bone.
There are so many sides to each shape.
Try to grasp the sand on the beach
between my toes
You may think whatever you like.
I know when I walk down your streets
you won't know who I am
and you'll pass me by.
You think you know it all
and I commend you for your brilliance.
You know how to say bye
really well,
and how to make me stop breathing
while you read my last ode to you.

Unwritten

Coffee cup on my notebook,
words in my head.
Tiny light to fill the darkness
as the owl in me
waits for the new
arrival of your suitcase,
with fresh linens to
exchange the old ones.
You behind the camera lens,
a kiss trembling from our lips,
give me something to still
the moment
but the poetry sucks
me in like a vortex,
leads me to that place
we can only see.
No one is there
but us,
writing and
rewriting our story.
Erasing
and creating,
pretending it never happened,
while my body and soul
cries how my essence is yours.
As pure as my blood,
it needs you
to drive the force
deep inside.
Walk away fast,
ignore me,
I'm too weak for you.
I knew you would go first.

Star

I want to hold you in the palm of my hand,
feel your sharpness
and see your points and valleys.
I want to possess you
but you are so far from my reach,
so far from my touch
that I cannot see your depth anymore.
You never surprise me—
constant,
wandering,
invisible,
as much as I try to enter your space
with telepathic thoughts
and technological vices.
You take way too long
to see tiny me here at this crossroad,
at this empty street
waiting for your light
to fill my soul
with a little bit of heaven.
I like to watch you so close
to my moon,
where my constellations
await
you to connect me together.
But you float away
and let me be,
hence I named you
after a dead poet.

Exit You Missed

I await so crazily
for the instant look of friendliness,
and we talk about the weather
and whether you would like
sugar and cream
or anything else with your coffee,
and you always search for
something new I have or
show me your latest book
and ask have I read it.
Do I like the characters
and what possesses them to
act so passionately,
and why couldn't we
just do whatever we liked to do—
never work,
never grocery shop,
never stop for milk and cigarettes,
never rent another movie,
never wait for the discounts?
Wouldn't life be so great
without rage and worry
about tomorrow's deadlines
and yesterday's debts.
Of course, you mention
that the sun is out today
and the terrace is so inviting
but the awful punch clock sound
awaits us,
not the view of downtown
and loud voices or people watching.
Wow, we can be loyal
to everyone else but our own self.

Do we have the moment to reflect
upon our desires and needs
or the time to definitely
follow through?

The children have to be fed
then bathed.
The dishes have to be washed,
the grease is sticky after two days.
The clothes are starting to smell
and I forgot my wallet at the bank.
Oh yeah, the grass is constantly growing,
the garden neglected,
the illusions of grandeur
laid out in a magazine of the latest trend.

Acquisitions surround me and become my extension.
That mirror from Spain
reflects castanets and guitars.
That carpet from Tanzania,
the desert dwellers are chanting
a rhythm so pure of honesty and torture
united among all outcasts.
The 1912 edition of *Alice in Wonderland,*
given to me by you,
is alive with imagination—
inspiration to do grand things
before forty approaches
like an exit you missed.

The heartbreak of this love sustains us
to continue driving to work,
stopping for a midnight snack,
or thoughts of a midnight run
to another highway.

We abandon our future
with these scribblings of a remote time
left unscathed
in an old torn notepad,
placed in some forgotten box
sealed under yellowed tape
and unseen by human eyes.
To read these personal emotions
of wanting to kiss you
every day
and never having the nerve
to even say how beautiful you
look to my almond-shaped eyes.

Voices

I woke up to the voices again,
after all that drinking and Saint-Henri parking
in front of the usual side streets
with bearded hipsters,
open door lofts,
stolen dreams. Coming out
of Cayenne and Pepper,
sexy shoes and leather.
I don't know what I was
thinking when we had those
shots, those drinks,
wine. And I didn't smash
into you at the street
corner, looking like
quite the classy whore.
There was some white lace too,
enough of it to want to see
underneath. No more questions
about my ass,
my poems.
Just listen to my voices,
or ignore me.
It's what you do best.
I ran out of cream,
have to always catch
myself as I fall. My arms
are comforting.
My words free me.
It's the only way
to breathe from the place
you make it hard to breathe from.
What distance? You're here.
What time? You're on it.

What sky? You're staring at it.
What sex? We did it.
Did you have enough of me?
Trust me, I know,
I have had just about enough
of myself too. I can't blame you
for leaving me, I wanted it.
It's my island,
I want to be alone
on it.

Those Familiar Leaves

Once again the leaves turn their autumn colors,
but without you to rake them.
Only a year ago we were running to the hospital,
searching for parking
and sharing our Second Cup coffee
with you.
We searched for your different room numbers
on various floors
where you barely ate
and doctors barely spoke.
You slowly ceased to move your limbs,
powerful legs that kicked soccer balls
where the eye could not see.
A mind that spoke so many truths
is left speechless
but not thoughtless.
They flowed through you.
We had to interpret
but could never comprehend
the swirls and bounds of your emotions.
Tears rolled down your cheeks,
pain looked straight into ours,
yet still
you did not
complain.
You ran up until
that hill was too high.
You counted up to forty-five
as I bent and stretched your body parts.
You rubbed your head
in that familiar way
we took for granted.
We tried to save you

but nothing can change
the turning of the leaves
to red-orange.
No internet concoctions,
solutions,
no pills
could have pulled you out
of the drowning pool
surrounding you.
Now the wind sends the leaves
to different directions
as you are overlooking
and never changing again.
You left us breathless,
homeless,
fighting the weather.
Now we step on the colorful leaves
as we walk to your new home.
We pour water on your daffodils
and light your candle,
enflame the incense,
kiss your porcelain photo
and embrace the cold tombstone.
We try to pull you near
to us,
but further away you seem
with each passing leaf,
falling around your name.

Ninety-Seven Years

You are gone from this life
and enter another one
where you will meet your brothers,
sisters,
wife,
grandchildren
who you have not seen in decades.
Maria will embrace you,
welcome you,
for she misses
the bickering, arguing,
the exchanges of sarcasm
as much as you miss her—
that not even the pills,
the long walks to the cafeteria,
could erase her from your mind.
You saw her everywhere you went
and had fantastic conversations
with her spirit.
Now you are home
after ninety-seven years
of music, of walking,
of counting money,
late-night eating,
TV watching.
After stories upon stories
of war and famine,
fairy tales of lost men and women,
story-telling nights
in one-room apartments,
honey-dipped butter and bread treats,
wine stashed in bureau drawers.
And let us not forget your dancing feet,

operatic voice,
and sense of humour—
unequalled and untouchable.
You were a spiritual being
chanting to God,
teaching us all
how to be lively,
grateful,
and simultaneously eccentric.

Even in your confused state
you joked about
the lady next to you
or
the old man down the
hall, making us laugh
like you always do—
so easily,
so uniquely
you.
In my mind,
I am two-years-old
and you are holding me.
Click.
A snapshot of a moment
placed in a photo album
but locked in my heart.

Peace
is finally in you,
you have fled
from this tragic life.
Good bye *Pappou*,
thank you for
the late-night knocks on my wall,

the music in you,
buying me my first camera,
and I especially thank you
for the hot cup of *krasi*
all those sick nights.

An Ode to Steve

One day you were alive and well,
casting everyone under your magic word spell.
Suddenly, you were no longer here
walking, talking, sharing a beer.
You were asleep for three weeks,
we wondered if you could hear our words
as we kissed your cheeks,
rubbed your hands,
sang you songs
from your favorite rock and roll bands.
We recounted the stories of forgotten years,
from little kids in Outremont with grown up fears,
to late night phone calls
about childhood, innocence, philosophy
and unbroken walls.

The soul of an angel is floating around us,
as tears and memories drown us
with the cute, funny way you said our names,
connecting us to you in a unique way.
Your different voices,
the way you said,
"Chrissy, has the laugh of an angel."
Childhood friends are mourning,
family is left empty without a warning,
hope has vanished into the great ocean,
as a brilliant mind
remains in our thoughts
of all those irreplaceable conversations,
the epiphanies, the heartbreak.
But
you are free now,
as we are caged

in this despair
of sleepless nights
and the never ending film of our life together,
and how we will live it now
without your laughter
to fill up the room.

Missing

A broken trampoline no one has the energy or desire to repair.
An unfinished manuscript of a book of poetry.
Hospital corridors are inviting me in,
rolling out their majestic red carpet.
My grandfather sees all the dead people
and the old lady down the hall
is creeping me out with her unblinking eyes.
A bulletin board of endless years
is what remains concrete now,
all the home-made cookies left untouched.
Cranberry juice, pills, and sleep
are his entrance steps into the imminent gates
where he sees his dead brother
telling him to milk the cows,
suck the egg whites from the fresh eggs—
it makes you strong and alive, he says, as he fades away.

His singing voice is not forgotten.
His memory somehow intact, yet
slowly vanishing into the pungent,
urinal smell surrounding him.
We reintroduce ourselves every day,
wait for one sense of recollection.
We grasp it, as tears roll from
our eyes. A kiss on a frail cheek,
but he wants us to stay the night.
Where will we sleep, he ponders over
and over. We are in his village now
we are flying home. I say nothing.
How can I tell him my car is parked
outside? We are in Canada. And the
children are not allowed to jump
on his bed and although he calls them

different names, he is pleased to
see them. His eyes light up. How I
hate to flee from this sad room.
He breathes, the nurse tells me
how sweet he is, and I smile.

In My Own Flood

It was a crisp autumn night. We changed
the course of our history. We lit
up the night with the stars in our eyes.
A thousand ships sailed by. Still. We
did not look away. I tried to drink my
cosmo slow. I tried to not peek at your
hands. But nothing I tried, worked.
I'm drowning in my own flood of words.
Can you still see me or have I faded out?
Hope and hockey hold hands in love and I
think about you. All the fucking time.
You did it. You made me want you when I
didn't even try. You said nothing about me
was common, and other phrases that kept
me awake. Running to the moon, right before
sunrise. Your words are ingrained like
photos in a wallet. A lost love. Art. Habit.
I should insist more but I like to drive
fast and sing along to your favorite song,
wear your favorite perfume.
But the most impressive part of this book
is how it showed me how to find myself in between
those realms you never looked.

NYC 2013

I see your face everywhere
and no where.
I feel your presence
colliding
and invading mine
I hear your voice
passing right by me.
I am not waiting
for the fusion.
Time is fleeting
in this hotel,
my leg up against a wall
waiting for my friends to
come.
Words are what keep
me standing on the street corner
looking up,
while you are looking down.
My scent gets lost
in the smog and smoke
of a never-ending city
with winding passages
and gloomy faces.
Love is whatever
makes you feel
invincible
omnipresent
constant.
Aye, my friend,
within our souls
are all the answers,
but who will take a peek
at it?

Who will see the Real You ever again
in the dark?
Maybe you will be lucky,
while I ponder stones
and shop for books.
Maybe you never saw me.
New York is a big city
and we hardly exist
do we?

So Feverishly

You call my house and I run,
run to hear you say
anything, whatever comes to mind.
I hear only you
and wish to talk to only your voice,
miles away from mine.
You feel nothing for me.
You will not pull my hair back
to kiss my perfumed neck.
I have caught your
desire, staring at me when you thought
I was not looking.
With your well performed role
of great friend
and of a lost, untouchable lover,
you cover it up well.
It must be easier this way
to have never wrapped my arms
around your back,
never looked at your naked torso,
never fought over
grocery lists and overdraft bank accounts.
All this turmoil
makes you act surprised to be near me.
I know the boiling kettle inside you is
yearning to comprehend my limits,
my zones of pleasure.
"Listen," I quietly whisper,
"You will never know
I am changing before you
to someone you never thought
you would crave
so feverishly."

You tell me to read between the invisible lines,
alive in front of us,
trying to trample on the lies
kept quiet,
lying in the cupboard.
Would you like to bake that delicious cake
you liked so much?
Chocolate and pecans
with a hint of banana.
You came over for coffee.
We never brewed it.
Our clothes evaporated
at the entrance door
before we even said
hello. I wore it for you.

One Thing

I am running out of lined paper
to express to you my visions
of an endless ocean between us,
and a magical connection
illuminating the light which is so distant,
unattainable.
Somehow I see you standing next to the post
waiting for my car to approach,
and my eyes to meet yours
so I can just say one more thing:
I imagine us running so far and so alone,
no one can stop this touch of our skin—
close, electrifying,
and still.
Still as a curtain with no open window
to feel a breeze.
Still as a lamp on a table,
only able to move by a human push or touch.
Come and see how still I am,
and wake me up to a new morning
where I see your naked back
and rustled hair.
Where we drink out of the same coffee cup
and I will certainly walk toward you
and tell you about my day,
and let us discuss Ulysses
and Javert and Heathcliff's
undying love for Catherine.
I know I said I would only tell you one thing,
but it seems I cannot stop writing
and exploding with emotions, stories, and heartbreak.
I can talk to you like this forever,
no response is necessary.

Just this paper and pen—
my company and my witness
to the bridge connecting my words to yours.
Could it be I hear a voice
so low, so quiet,
reaching over to whisper something?
But I hear the music is too loud,
and I once again
imagine this sailboat riding over the Aegean Sea,
drowning me.

Shades

When the shades are drawn,
the quiet of the night befriends me.
This is the part you enter
like a guest I have been cooking for.
Your image stays the same,
body never changes,
but you fall down from exhaustion.
You are too heavy for my light arms,
I cannot carry you
so I speak to you instead.
I tell you that you have the most
peculiar eyes I have ever seen.
I am a mind reader.
Suddenly
the dark is no longer flawed,
it appears to be entangled in ashes
and upside down wine bottles.

I may not know your favorite color
but we are not eight.
Do I really care about those trivial things?
I should,
but the tombstone is behind me now
while you are up high in your white chemise.

As soon as I see your laugh lines
I forget the tone of your voice
and your favorite expressions.
So I accept my solitude,
embrace the ashtray,
and turn empty bottles right side up.

How I Fell From The Sky

Naked and alone
like the Terminator
scrunched up in some goddess-like pose.
Fear and pain
like a refugee girl
leaving behind her home.
The moon and the sun
had my back
they protected my aura
for a while
until I had to face the hurricane
and get swept by your tornado
but what left me helpless
between the clouds
was when your plane flew
under me.
You thought of me
and I saw your eyes
were not vacant at all.
They could not see mine
of course, last time
you saw me I was on the ground
dead from your departure
so up until the tsunami
of your love
drew me back from the universe
that was when I knew
it was time
to come back to you
as you looked up
and spread your arms wide
to catch my tiny frame
and that is how
I fell from the sky.

Follow Up Poem

To the one I wrote a while back
about our trip where tears
wrecked the drive as you threw
words at me like darts.
I meant to keep quiet
but I can't bite my own tongue
I have to tell you how roller coaster rides
are not my thing, how being alone with me
is a dreamy fantasy.
Real life is such a drag
and time ticks the loudest
when you have to leave me
the slowest when you kiss my cheeks.
I cherish moments
like seashells
pluck them out for warmth
on a cold spring Montreal morning
when I am searching out the best
cafe latte and Olympico has a lineup
so I undo my button
to meet you
but boobs are overrated these days
even natural ones
and legs are only sexy
when you can touch them
and tiny walls are only holding me up
when I am lonely.
I met my maker
in the bathroom
and locked myself
in on purpose.
I get nervous when I see you
and I can't hide my feelings
ever

I am not a good liar
at all
I don't have a poker face
and
frankly, I give such a damn
about you
it scares me.

Four

It was painful, but what hurt the most
was not the physical pain. the scraping
of my uterus
reminds me of candles
not blown on a birthday cake.
of unknown names and faces
that haunt me.
that time, I wanted it to be taken,
convinced,
university mattered more than life.
the second time, it was dead
before I looked down
to watch my tummy
grow.
the third time
it was a boy. and my dad
was alive to hold him.
the fourth time
it was a girl. at the
ultrasound I cried.
i held my breath
praying i would have
a daughter.
to replace being
a daughter. but that
is eternal too.
pinched with love
and Greek sayings.
So when the nurse asked me *how many children do you have*? I
    paused.
I really wanted to say four
but my husband
would not understand
how I think about
the other two
all the fucking time.
Two, I replied, a little breathless. a little jaded.

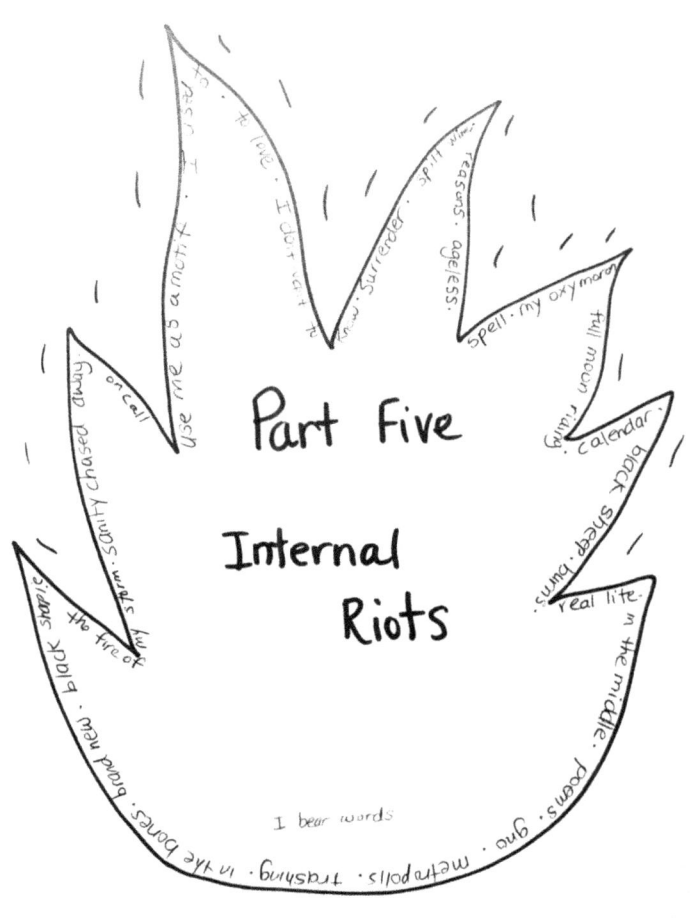

PART FIVE
Internal Riots

Use me as a motif

Listening to subscribed channels about loving myself
is probably more harmful than actually loving.
You can abandon people and they are still in the dark
even if I research the best methods of unloving someone
it can't be done. Rooms wait for people to walk into
and as long as I wait for you
you can't come in to see me. It's fine. I prefer it that way.

Death beds are beautiful places to end up in. Heaven
is a place you described once, while I wasn't in the room.
I can see you there talking to her and pretending
I don't exist. It's painful. It's not what I thought.
I'm absent from this part of the story.
You can use me up until I say no more.
It's coming. That day you dread. Death sucks up love
at will. You can go about your silence.
It has no guilt.

I used to

pour out my words here
but all these labels are too much
for any girl to handle. All these
late night drinking binges
are way out of my league.
I'm home
relaxed, pretending to not think of you
waking up before the alarm
with words and sex on my tongue.

It's only been fourteen days
of not loving you. The rest of it
does not count. I'm not here
anymore. I passed the highway
I sigh your name
yet, my feet are planted
on another dry ground.

It's not a writing competition
I'm not in the PTA
I am full of insecurities
I've shown you all my vulnerabilities
you snatch them up
throw them up
spit them out
as of that is the answer
to this mess.

When you read my mind
your adrenaline is hard
but my words
that's all I got
that's off topic
it's art

not you, not me
not my books
it's none of that.

Skin is difficult to touch
eyes are easy to read
songs are pleasant to send

everything is still misunderstood
off the shoulder tragic.

I'm so mad at you
after all these years
don't you know how I feel?
I love how you battle with words
and let time descend on you
like a vulture

I'm only unkind with words
when you let your monster out
your inner soul
becomes an unattainable star
it has no future
in this life
only a hidden past.

To Love

Did you forget what it feels like to love?
You would prefer to hate your own history

blame me for all your wrongdoings.

I am an open dart and your hands
the weapon. You did not forget
      you pretend
to not love me. I see through it.
I lay down awake
but I am a cliché, dead inside.
I cried and you watched me
sending others to comfort me
while you left
silence destroyed us once again.

I knew this would happen
I am a witch after all. Love
has a way of pulling you apart
when you close it down.
I can detach, this is my power.
I can run, this is my mission.
I can order for two
and only be one.
All the love you promised
I mopped it away
with the urine stains.
Did you forget what it feels like to love?
I can no longer remind you,
for I forgot.
I do answer my own questions
I am a poet after all
and my typewriter needs me.

I don't want to know

It's been such a long time
I haven't seen your face
maybe you do not believe
in the same books anymore
or philosophers
or artists
or punctuation.

I see a garden stopped growing
journal overflowed with moss

I give up on this whole
we got so much time
because we don't.

Time soaks with truth
keeps on creating death
to remind us
we won't live forever
even if you sing about it.

Brand New

Every dress she wore
had a hole in it. She used to sew
but they always came apart,
she was never as good as
her grandmother. Now it is
a stand she takes
to breakdown the hold he has
on her waist
on her tight fitting dress
on her immaculate heart
she refuses to make it
brand new
preferring the tattered one
for it is the perfect shade of faded black
she paid 500 hundred dollars
still has the receipt.
Everyone knows she loves
that old dress,
his jacket covers her moles.
He could buy her more
but having names on her ass
means nothing to her
if it is not poetry.
She believed in old hockey cards,
the ones she found in his attic,
The Rocket
close to his heart,
she competed with dead hockey players
he competed with dead poets.
She found his hockey skates
in a dusty milk crate dated 1977
an expo hat that his uncle
from Greece left behind one year he visited

in a rush to get back to his olive trees.
He found nothing of hers
this pained her
this idea that he would discover
her soul in death,
this burial of all her poems
only to be unearthed by him.
If only she had driven him that night
he would be here
reading her words
and not under the frozen earth

and she
using words like
forever
always
and meaning them.

Black Sharpie

Sometimes I sense my inked heart
is as dark as black coffee
filled with typed lies,
other times
it's hurtful silence
or a cream light
filled with the plastic of the earth
or the picked flowers rotting in a vase.

Sometimes I read people
like a reread book
other times I cut up my poems
and make new ones out of old words.

Surrender

The line up for free coffee
is growing daily
up until they too
take away the free love.
Not something I am unaccustomed to
all I crave is
my surrender to your clever ways
play me anyway
I'm game
raising flags at red lights
stopping my heart from breathing
to feel yours
hiding away under the life machines
holding onto technology
like doctors
who are poets in their own way
as we are
saving lives with words.
It seems redundant to write
how you have the words
I want whispered in my ear
caressing my skin
and all the other ordinary words
literature stems from
but 'tis true. Yes.
Shakespeare is in love again.
I found these words scattered
around six in the morning
where my notebook lay empty.
I raise my love to you
and bore you to death
with my obsessions
and that is how easily
you can forget me

you are the air
I am of the earth
and this another reason
I will surrender
for
both
need each other
more than they know
it could be science
it could be love
it could be none of the above.

The Fire of my Storm

Inside my chest
is a raging child
she buckles up her seat belt
and waits for the accident
it comes
it always does.

I remember her at six
how the piano freed her soul
anger burned her wings
in burial grounds
where her mother met her fate.

This storm inside her at sixteen
tore apart all her friendships
those addictions to people
taught her about toxicity
before the definition became a trend.

Now at thirty-four
she sleeps alone
waits for the shores
of her youth to be taken
by the roads she missed.

She is a torturous wave
waiting for her destiny
her own white lightning.

Spilt Wine

Start the night with wine
in my hair, on my dress,
in my stockings
sparkling new red shoes
bare skin
over the shoulder top
and a few half-muttered apologies.
I saw it coming too
watched it like a film reel
I'm the main actress
like life
that was yesterday
tonight,
now another bar
singing the blues
under copper tiled ceilings
and feathers in the singer's hair
you'd think it was 1920
art deco Paris
but no
it's the house of Jazz
in Laval, Quebec
hanging with the girls
who sold my life away
Do you pay the bill?
cosmos and red chandeliers
blue bottle in the vitrine
it's a dreamy colorful world
in here
the only thing missing is you
it makes me lose perspective
what I see
you'll never see it

not even these lame photos
do it justice

Rita called me
She'll be twenty minutes late
goddamn Montreal traffic she texts
I order another cosmo
write this poem on my phone
listen to the jazz singer
and lament
you
as if
everytime we see each other
is the final goodbye.

Reasons

Some people love you
for all the right reasons
but you still go searching
for the wrong ones. The ones
that keep you up or make you
want to smoke all day.
I never hide behind a persona
or a brand
I am what I am
sometimes ditsy
sometimes brilliant
but always me. I woke up
in a Woody Allen movie
you can guess the title
you know it's dysfunctional
and petty
yet narcissistic. I liked
talking to you
you never interrupt
this is such a quality
I adore. I don't have
scorn, I love you
I put up these walls
to protect myself
from how much I care.
I will never tell you
or maybe
if I'm drunk
and Purple Rain's solo
comes on the speakers
and you see me
turn to me with your eyes
tell me

how you never meant
to cause me any sorrow
I know I am smarter
than you think. I carry
you like e.e cummings' poem
nowadays
it's modern
in my phone
in my pocket
but in another era
it was in my heart
and you
you are invisible to everyone
but me. You are like
a magician
popping into my life
like the pills I swallow.
I loved and lost
you
in true poet fashion

between the lines of a poem

you can't get
any closer to art
than a few hours
alone
in a locked room.

Sanity Chased Away

Rain clouds have stories you've been
waiting to hear
melodies you've only heard in your dreams
for without chances and change
we can be a living corpse
even the truth can't change your feelings
sometimes you have to go under
for a fresh breath of air.

It's not you, it's me
that classic bullsit line
we use when we want to be polite
to our heartbreak

all these years
I believe in wrong expressions.

That's why adages take walks
I can understand them in a forest
I have to think way too hard
analyze words in ways
my mind cannot reach

about the English Language
when I'm more comfortable in Greek
under the earth with my father
drowning in planted seeds.

I want to be here
writing in my kitchen
alone.
No one talk to me
no one to break my zone of silence.

I'm bonding with words now
my one true connection

you get me high on you
I will not turn away from you

I will not ever see you again
this, I understand
but
words
well, they always are my warm drink
my safe place

even without your voice
telling me otherwise.

Ageless

I know that age matters not
right now
but then it did.
It mattered when we raced against
the wind. I was just a babe in your arms.
You were a man even as a teenager.
You had this way of bringing me love
on a tray, and spoiling me until
I was full of your love. I had it
all, for a brief time. I showed you
my healing cuts and blue bruises
you kissed them with earthly lips.
Your singing mouth on my shoulder
my hands unbuckling your belt
such a frantic youthful way
in an ageless time
between this world and the next
and the past one.
let's remember where we were
recall the age of Us
it matters that you see past the girl.
We felt invincible
will never know that freedom again
that youthful love
we hold onto
with natural grips
of nostalgia.

Spell

I want to be silenced with kisses
upon kisses that take away all the emptiness
in some loud downtown club
with glass and hope
where we can't even hear ourselves speak
the music is more important
than conversation
who wants to talk anyway
about
how miserable life is
how hopeful you want it to be
how people think all this is real
how ikea is lonely
all this magic and no one
to cast a spell
on me. All this truth and no one
to say it to. All these lies and
no one to bullshit to.
I will always want you
that is what souls do
when they connect
they have this memory
we can't keep track of
and in the middle of the day
when you are on the way
to this or that place
you place your face against
the dashboard in your car
listening to the same song on repeat
ignoring incoming calls of
where the fuck are you
and trying to find tissues
in some random parking lot

where other strangers seem to be doing
what you are

suddenly you don't feel so alone

holding on
tired of the rush
the age is becoming an issue
time, it is entering my notions
of what I could never be
such idiotic thoughts
I can never hide from
no amount of clubs
will stop the mind

kiss me quickly
ease the internal battle of doubt

I may not say it enough
but I love you

all the things I do
mean I love you

all the things I don't do for you
mean I love you even more

and you never notice
how passionately I can love someone
who keeps on leaving.

On Call

Waiting for the tiles
5.99 a sq foot
trunk is open
boxes are filled up with colors
of the future
zen me up to Buddha
he has my grout
in an abundance of worthless forests
I came upon myself
while you were shouting
how bad I am at everything I do
and that's when I knew
I am not ever going to get
the kind of love
I need

I write you out of my life
but you know every button
that makes me weak
my switches
to turn me on.

I hate this love
I am crazy
for cement
I need no sky
I am feeling worthless
please leave
my self-esteem out of this
my poem is about
how no man or woman
should be together for long
moments are what I can count
on my fingers now
mostly bad ones.

Making Love Vs Fucking

If you want to know the truth
I think you meant to make love to me
but your body wanted to fuck
you started off with honey black kisses
and a lover with a dark heart
need only fucking
to drive away the making love.
You say making love
to appease the romantic in me
the truth is you're just another man
ready to fuck
with his body full
and his mind on my ass,
it's fine
honestly, I am guilty
of fucking myself
and making love is so far
from my mind
that I left the rose petals
in my book.
If you want to make love
let's talk about it
if you want to fuck
let's be silent
I went in a circle
from one extreme to the other
but we all know
fucking and making love
have fine lines in the sand
and only a few know
the difference.

My Oxymoron

Drowning on cement
while no one
sees the ocean but me
I feel the salt on my skin
alongside your imaginary kisses.
Many women and men
would die to be
in our position
we can write with our eyes closed
our hearts bare
ready to be diagnosed
analyzed. I can write
with my legs spread wide
and your pen on my thighs.
I can breathe better behind
the typewriter
less sighs
more moans
I wish I could never leave
this place. It makes me weary
to have to stop writing
and continue on with life.
Must I really eat?
Live inside one room?
Must I talk to people I dislike?
Below my surface
there are no categories
or boundaries. Below my
waist there are your hands
grasping tightly
As I run away.
I can join teams but
I am always solo

in my thoughts.
This photo of me
is not really me
I lied
      I am not who I am
I made it up
and no amount
of talking
can hide the tears
I see falling from the skies
I'm a big tiny
      poet
with no more pens
in my closet.

Full Moon Riding

I felt the full moon
creep up
wink at me
as if it holds secrets
to the commoner
who goes to work
who does not look up
at its reflection
5:42 it will be there
our time
don't snap a photo
keep it to yourself
you whisper to keep it real
I know most of you
will be busy
driving through traffic
picking up your kids
racing home to cook dinner
taking out the trash
unaware and uninvited to this gala
Who cares? You say
but I do, of course
and that man I met in another life
and maybe that woman you once loved
and can't get out of your mind
and maybe that man I let touch my panties
in the middle of the day
so many and, buts, and ifs
to contemplate at the traffic lights
everyone hopes this poem is about them
but don't be silly
this poem is and will always be about me.

Calendar

It's just another day on your calendar
to pick up a cup of coffee
on your way to work

big decision may be to decide upon
which coffeehouse?
which blend?
The news is skipping channels
but to me it's the anniversary
of my father's death

nine years have come and gone
I was weak in the knees upon
hearing he had seven months to live

get over it people may say
don't look at the past
be in the moment
but we all know
sadness is what the future holds

more than we ever imagined
more useless deaths
hate crimes
war
destruction of mother earth
lithium batteries
loved ones diagnosed
with more labels
to research

sitting here
in the waiting room once again

to find out if my breasts
hold life or death in them

how is that for being in the present

poets live in the moment
and write all about it for years

I would have come with you
I love you
he texts

everyone is so wrapped up
in their own calendar
filling in slots with words
neglecting you

it's just another day
of the unknown

life is supposed to be creative this way

lately, I'm empty
the well of words
running dry like a cliche in this poem

I go on and on
only to discover
more appointments
to change my life
into a new one

wanted or unwanted
most times
we don't have a choice

at least I have a view of the city
waiting in a white and pink flowered robe
breasts hanging
clothes hung in a stale room
waiting for me to leave

I don't feel sexy at all
in fact
I feel like a wilting flower
anticipating life
being taken away
in a split second
the way it usually happens

but the young doctor tells me
with his hipster beard and black rimmed glasses
you have dense breasts but nothing to worry about
see you in a year

I thank him get dressed in my tight jeans
black bra, lace panties
and wonder how one minute
I am almost dying in my mind
and the other I am ready
to text my ex-lover.

Black Sheep

It was such a long time ago
when you said there is a method
to my madness
and lyrics sounded sweet
coming from your parted lips

and poetry sounded epic
from your strong hands
it was such a long time ago
when you visited
me from your European swirl
begged me to stay
down on my knees

I believe in poetry
like a Catholic believes in Christ
I believed in you
like a woman in love
I lost some hope
when you became the black sheep
inside yourself

you said,
you have the art in you

I said,
silence waits for you

we destroyed our sanity
and it was not such a long time ago
that you loved me
and left me
for all the reasons you first loved me.

Burns

Nothing feels normal
when you love with an ache
in your chest. A longing
that can never be fulfilled
distance can be mathematically
calculated

it's so easy
to memorize the formula
of two cities
but emotionally inaccurate

I started off with coffee
ended with vodka
I try to be good
but I think of all the ways to be bad
especially with you

I do hate the feeling
of never seeing you
lost in illusions of hope
who knows if it will
happen again
quite so universally perfect

we can plan it
but I will lose my mind
and no one can tell
I'm not fine. I lost my innocence
a long time ago. You had
nothing to do with it
although you always seem to think you do.
Husbands and wives can be like that
think it is all about them

best time to leave for New York
is when you're young
as I did at sixteen
only I should have never
come back.

Real life

it takes a toll on you
to wake up
make breakfast
carry on like nothing
has changed you.
you're supposed to be the same
person you were yesterday
but so much can change in a day
alter your world
into a new dimension
the one you never imagined
you would be on

real life
can be a cloud filled with art
a denial up until
it weaves its way into
your world and captures
you in its net. You're caught
now. You can't shake your legs
or arms. You're stuck
swimming on earth
or drowning in hell
or both

Poets think they know
everything
with all the
chips on their shoulders
wearing them down
and their poor rejections
affirming
they know absolutely nothing

they live in dreams
real life is another
way of killing you slowly
without knives.

In the Middle

Once I was at the end of the love song crying for years because it was over before it even began
we were caught loving the wrong person and so I immersed from my drowning and swam to the beginning of the line
I sailed across your poems and floated on the abstract words you sent by mail, on out-dated vintage postcards, the kind you find in those tiny alcoves with low rent and bearded fools
you wrote them on the back of your hand with your fingertips
I sent you powdered magic and labyrinths with one needle on your arm while we lived in a movie and recited Shakespeare's sonnet 113 naked in bed arguing about the best imagery
you were not even close to being who I thought you were and I was too much for you to handle as you said
small doses of me like drops of rain
I climbed Mount Kilimanjaro in heels and you laughed at my absurdities because I was spontaneous, explosive, until I wasn't anymore
I bent backwards on words and the power of your hands on my skin turned me into a love song
now I'm in the middle of something that will change me forever
I will never be that girl again so I have to be someone I thought I would never be
life plants itself in your veins but we forget to drink water
our drought
placed in the hope of songwriters and poets
but for a regular woman like me
it's a waste of my time
I was never taught to be myself.

Poems

have some in my pocket
under my skirt
between my legs
along the highway to the city
writing them in my head
in my bed
everywhere but here

I'll come back sooner or later
but they take control now
and my notebooks aren't empty enough
and my love is not as full as I want it
so I drown in it
add some ice to it
and shake the shaker
with instant love cocktails on the table

I'm the best suburban downtown barmaid
around
my heart has roots
you look like sisters and other lies I hear
oh, come on, you know the drill
the midnight thrill
you can find it anywhere else
but here
poems set me aflame now
let reality burn down
to the ground
I won't call 911
I'd rather be a ghost
I see nothing but love
and even that covers itself up
and hides from this painting
leaves my blindfolds on

I like it that way.

GNO

Vodka, champagne
ice bucket
free drinks on the house
we know the club owner
we are the privileged friends
we drink and eat like the rich
pretend we mean something
to no one

girls
girls
girls
on fire
like the song
and the videos
impressed by shoes
purses
with not much to say

q & a for me

What do I think of a thousand dollar pair of shoes?

I had so much to say
and no one cared to listen
a few mumbled
she's a writer
hence the nods
at my philosophy of designer shoes
purses
panic if someone stepped on you
or spilled their drink on your purse
I am ready for the exit

but first I need a few more drinks
to discuss how I prefer to spend
a thousand dollars on books
and making my skin so thick
with words
no one can penetrate
and you won't catch me dead in those

I tell my stories
and a few listen
others ignore
the women are complimenting each other out loud
and then whispering the truth

my phone is cracked
the song turns into my favorite color

on the drive home my friend turns to me and says
you're just an oddity no one understands or gets you
so don't get angry because they don't know
you

I've known
you for years and I get it, but that girl who said

she knew you but never met you
she knew where you lived
she knew all about you
that was fucked up
she said nice to finally meet you

well, that could very well be a stalker

I swear the night just got stranger
by the hour

I could not wait to get the fuck out
and stop defending my art
my brand of shoes
my vegan food
my new colored hair
the title of my books
my erotic book
my art

I need to seriously be drunk before
I face a society of girls
or say no next time.

Metropolis

I mostly watched the singer
shake away his age
as it caught up with him
and nothing seemed to impress us
anymore besides one hundred dollar bills
and tequila shots. The youth left us
with our past. Our ten percent shot
at another night of bringing back the
good old bad days. All the drunken sailors
tried to get their hands on us
but we have to try much more now
and drink less
we are sick of the city
the plastic dirt
the envious eyes
we tire of the puddles
the back door hurt
the lack of flowers
the indecent potholes
the five-dollar coffee cups missed garbage cans
we are part of the fake news
the killing sprees
the hiding of ugly humanity
I swear I want to leave this city and never look back
you say
never think about what language I should speak first
second guess someone's authenticity
if I should say bonjour or hello

I like the vast sky
I reply

the view from the windows on my quiet street

I wanted to run from it and chase the night like a shot
now I want to sit
enjoy the kids playing hockey in the middle of summer
drink a cup of mint tea
plant an herbal garden
and never look back to who
I used to be before I met you.

Trashing

in the evening, Jack sings
as I wrap gifts
I get paint in my fingernails
no artificial colors here
you talk about me as if
I am not in the room
as if
I can't hear or read
what with all my diplomas
certificates
licenses
degrees
you'd think I would get more respect
but I listen to the same ol' songs tapping my foot
any time of day
jumping naked
on the bed
bra flung over your tie
panties long gone

Did you forget I write stories?
I invent scenes
acts in roman numerals
tragic characters

Did you forget I have a writing problem?
label me hypersensitive

crying over everything you say about me

I ignore for a second or two
and then I run

don't forget to bring milk, you shout
as my angry exit
turns into an errand

I grab my purse and keys

You're going out like that?

Yeah, fuck off I say in my head

but everything I invent
comes from somewhere.

fights
trash talk
bite me when I come back

with my bag of skim milk
tight jean shorts

you know you want to

the drive
the music
the wind
made me all better now

Don't you see?

I came here for you
I'll leave in spite of you
all you say
is you're not impressed with any of it
sell my life away
sell my thoughts

my peach bra
my almond eyes see it all

I forgot to make supper
I forgot your shirts at the dry cleaners

but I remember
how you touch me
while I sleep.

In the Bones

Most times I try to hide it under my grief
but when I think of how eleven years pass
and how scientifically the skin and body
becomes all bones and maggots
this makes me scream at the sky
I think of how his skin once touched mine
how his love made me feel completely human
most days, I struggle to get out of bed
feed my medical condition
hate the daylight
it sucks up my dreams
I hate the night
it eats up my words
spits out my worries
I hate locks
they control me
I know how my mind words
under this umbrella
it takes hold of all my bones
and caresses them while I live
you are not scared of death
he had told me
while lying there
dying from a freak accident
that he should never have had
it was my fault
I wanted him to get me a burger and fries
at eleven at night
on a slippery Montreal night
and the police officer said
all the things you never want to hear
while waiting for your husband
to bring you food
rubbing your belly.

I suppose that is why
I never eat meat now
to forget how toxic it can be.

I bear words

You'll see I'm going to make it, I said
you've been making it for years, he replied

wear my tie and nothing else
there I was back at the starting line
of twenty years prior

it's easy to love someone
who never stops loving you
who sees you every day
without the persona
the blue eye shadow
the unwritten metaphors

it's hard to give your soul to strangers
for a few days and get it right back
unharmed

you make it easy to disappear
you make it harder to come back

don't let the bastards grind you down
Atwood writes
Bono sings

I told a stranger I can start my own poetry club
without stars and retweets
favorites, likes
blocks
haters
so-called friends who block
stalk
track my sales
steal my poems

I can flee
but I'd rather watch you sleep

wake up to your I love you eyes
confuse all my realities

love and hate you in each life
murmur to my spirit guides

submit my life
in one hundred pages
to print and out of print presses
wear my bangs and old jeans
tighter and sexier
age matters not
to souls

you don't get that part of me
wrapped up
you need to get the scissors out
cut the ribbons

the bohemian long-skirted girl
who jumped over fences for you
to meet you under the dark skies.

You get that sweet spread your legs girl
the one that never rests

it's complicated to admit defeat
I bear words
swords with pills
I gulp philosophies
choke on western medicine
I fast for you
creeping long years

calendar months
fast-paced days

it keeps me sane
insane
but never common
or boring

so can you take back your words
that I can't regurgitate
the ones I hide under veils
of metaphors

the words I can never type

the ones that give me a writing problem

No, you can't take them back
I know
I am being immature

I bear them all
like a witch about to be hung
the woman I was in a past life
the one you never met.

I keep dying and living
healing people.
A healer in every life
with words inside my bones
poems under my veins
a flood of sentences
surrounding my body
like a warm blanket
during a freezing Montreal winter.

I bear words for you.

ACKNOWLEDGEMENTS

I want to thank my husband Greg, my children and my family and friends for believing in me. My mother, my father, for giving me the freedom to be me.

I would like to thank my niece Tina, who took my phone in 2016 and created an Instagram account for me, created my username and gave me the inspiration to reach a whole new audience and hence write this book.

In this second edition, I added Part Five, which is entirely new. These poems are from my blog and have never been published before in any of my books.

Last summer, during Covid, I decided to rewrite all of the poems from my Wordpress blog. I discovered an entire community of writers who helped me grow as a poet and supported my work on Wordpress. I wrote these poems on a daily basis from the tip of my fingers straight into a post and published them immediately. They were not edited or mulled over. It was a pure stream of consciousness. The poems in this collection are from my early period. There are hundreds of poems I wrote this way, at that time. I hope to rewrite them all and put them in another book.

Lastly, I want to thank the Universe for being a part of my existence and giving me inspiration on a daily basis.

Please come visit me and say hello:

www.christinastrigas.com
Twitter: @christinastriga
Facebook: Christina Strigas Author
Instagram: c.strigas_sexyasspoet
email: christinastrigasauthor@gmail.com

ABOUT THE AUTHOR

Christina Strigas is an author and poet, raised by Greek immigrants. She is from Montreal, Quebec.

Her fifth poetry book, *for all the lonely hearts being pulled out of the ground*, was recently published by Free Lines Press.

Her books can be found at all online bookstrores.

In her spare time, Christina enjoys foreign cinema, reading the classics, and cooking traditional Greek recipes that have been handed down from her grandmother. She also likes to create her own herbal tea remedies.

If You enjoyed this poetry book
please leave a review
Let me know what you think.

Share your favorite poems on social media
or lend the book to friends.

Thank you for spending time with my book.
I wish you all love & Light.

May the source be with you.

CHRISTINA STRIGAS

www.ingramcontent.com/pod-product-compliance
Lightning Source LLC
Chambersburg PA
CBHW070427010526
44118CB00014B/1931